Funny You Should Ask

How to Make Up Jokes and Riddles with Wordplay

by Marvin Terban

Illustrated by John O'Brien

Clarion Books
New York

To the memory of my dear mother
SARAH TERBAN
who always loved a good joke.

Clarion Books
a Houghton Mifflin Company imprint
215 Park Avenue South, New York, NY 10003
Text copyright © 1992 by Marvin Terban
Illustrations copyright © 1992 by John O'Brien

Library of Congress Cataloging-in-Publication Data

Terban, Marvin.
Funny you should ask : how to make up jokes and riddles with
wordplay / by Marvin Terban.
p.   cm.
Summary: Offers an abundant cache of ideas about using words and
wordplay to create engaging riddles and jokes.
ISBN 0-395-60556-3. — ISBN 0-395-58113-3 (pbk.)
1. Riddles, Juvenile.   2. English language—Homonyms—Juvenile
humor.   3. Play on words—Juvenile literature.   [1. Puns and
punning.   2. Riddles.   3. English language—Homonyms.   I. Title.
PN6371.5.T433   1992   91-19509
808.7—dc20   CIP   AC

BP   10 9 8 7 6 5 4 3 2 1

Contents

The Joke's on You!

Everybody loves a funny joke or riddle. But have you ever wondered what makes jokes funny? Very often it's wordplay—words playing with each other and with you.

This book will introduce you to four of the most common kinds of jokes that people laugh at every day:

jokes with homonyms (sound-alike words),
jokes with almost-sound-alike words,
jokes with homographs (words with more than one meaning),
jokes with idioms (common sayings).

This book will also help you to spot the wordplay that makes a joke or riddle funny. You'll learn how to use these playful words to make up jokes and riddles of your own. Now you can be the life of the party, or your classroom, or your camp, or your club, or your living room, or wherever you want to be.

Are you ready to have your funnybone tickled? Are you ready to learn how to tickle someone else's funnybone? What this world needs is more good laughs. The world is counting on you. Let's go!

° 1 °

Jokes with Sound-Alike Words

There are hundreds of words in English that sound exactly like hundreds of other words. They're spelled differently. They have different meanings. But they sound exactly the same. In school your teacher may call these words homonyms or homophones. Here are some examples you might hear or read every day:

hoarse and *horse*   *tacks* and *tax*
bare and *bear*   *steal* and *steel*
which and *witch*   *not* and *knot*

You can use pairs (or sometimes triplets) of sound-alike words to make up jokes and riddles. By the way, a riddle is just a joke written as a trick question ("the straight line") and a funny answer ("the punch line").

Let's try it. Take the familiar words *fowl* and *foul*. They are homonyms because they sound alike but are spelled differently and mean different things. *Fowl* refers to a bird like a chicken, duck, or turkey. *Foul* means dirty or not according to accepted standards.

Now let's try to make up some jokes by playing with these words. Think of situations in which a bird (fowl) is doing something that is filthy or unacceptable (foul). The humor will come from switching one sound-alike word for another in a way that's unexpected and funny.

Remember, there are different ways of phrasing a joke. You might come up with a newspaper headline, a bit of conversation with lines of dialogue, a question and answer, a riddle, or a one-liner.

Headline:　　CHICKENS ARRESTED
　　　　　　　FOR FOWL PLAY!

Mama Hen: I'm going to wash your beak out with soap.
Baby Chick: Why, Mama?
Mama Hen: Because you used fowl language.

What did the chicken hit in the baseball game?
A fowl ball.

"Where's that handsome baseball player, Ronald
Rooster?"
"He's out with four fowls!"

Did you hear about the farmer who sprayed his
chickens with perfume because he couldn't stand
the fowl smell?

Which *fowl / foul* joke is the best? It's the one that
you (and your friends) think is the funniest.

As you can see, there's often more than one way to make up a joke using the same sound-alike words. Experiment with variations on your jokes. Try different versions out on different people until you get the biggest giggles, yuks, chuckles, and guffaws.

Ready for another exercise in joke-making? Take *roll* (a round portion of bread) and *role* (a part in a play or movie). Stretch your imagination. Think of ways to combine an acting part (role) with a small loaf of bread (roll) in the same context or situation. By playing with these homonyms a little, you can create joke variations like these:

She: I was in the movie *The Breakfast Club.*
He: Really?
She: Sure! I had a big roll.

She: I was in the movie *Invasion of the Hamburger Bun.*
He: You were?
She: Yup! I had a meaty roll.

She won an Academy Award for her part in the movie *The Stale Bread.* She played a hard role.

"I was in the movie *Breakfast at Tiffany's.*"
"Did you have a big role?"
"No, just an English muffin."

Now let's roll along.

Take the triple homonyms *scents*, *cents*, and *sense*. Think of funny situations in which you could substitute one word for another. Play with ideas like odors, aromas, perfumes (scents), pennies, coins, money (cents), and smart thinking, good judgment, and wisdom (sense). You might come up with jokes like:

Why did the inventor destroy his perfume-making machine?
It didn't make scents.

Headline: INVENTOR DESTROYS
          PENNY-MAKING MACHINE!
          IT DIDN'T MAKE CENTS.

If only part of a word sounds like another word, you can use it to make up more jokes. For example, if you replace *sens* in sensational with *scents*, *cents*, or *sense*, you can come up with jokes like:

Bob: I just won a million dollars!
Rob: That's sensational!
Bob: In pennies.
Rob: That's cents-ational.

"This new perfume smells like roses, violets, and oranges."
"That's scents-ational!"

Here are more jokes with the same idea.

A person who is allergic to pennies is very cents-itive!

or

A person who is allergic to perfume is very scents-itive!

"Why do you buy such expensive perfumes?"
"I want to be the scenter of attention."

Teacher: If your eyes are on the top of your face, and your mouth is at the bottom, where is your nose?
Little kid: The scenter.

The variations are almost endless. And in their own comical way, they actually make sense.

Sometimes you can stretch your joke-making possibilities by matching one word with a two-word phrase that sounds like it, for instance:

diet and *dye it*   *lettuce* and *let us*
illegal and *ill eagle*   *tulips* and *two lips*
ketchup and *catch up*   *toupee* and *to pay,*

as in the following jokes.

A lady who had gained a little weight was trying on her favorite dress. "It doesn't fit right anymore," she complained.
"You'll have to diet," said her husband.
"What color?" asked his wife.

Law professor: What's the difference between *unlawful* and *illegal*?
Student: *Unlawful* is against the law. *Illegal* is a sick bird!

Two tomatoes were racing to the hamburger bun. One fell behind but said he'd ketchup later.

Phil: Should we order a green vegetable?
Phyllis: Yes—lettuce!

What flowers are under your nose?
Tulips!

Sign in store that sells men's hairpieces:
"We accept cash or checks. How do you want
toupee?"

Not all jokes have to be hilariously funny to be good. Every joke doesn't have to make you laugh so hard that your stomach aches and tears roll down your cheeks. Some may just make you smile. Others may make you groan because they're such awful puns. But those can be fun, too.

Since there are hundreds of homonym pairs in English, there are hundreds of funny possibilities. In this chapter you'll find more than two dozen of them. On page 20, the homonyms in each joke and riddle are revealed. Have fun!

1. What was the rabbit's ring made out of?
   14 carrot gold.

2. What did the moose call his girlfriend?
   Deer.

3. Geography teacher: Who knows where the Great Plains are?
   Student: At the big airports.

4. When the housekeeper went to Tokyo for vacation, she left the following note: "Maid in Japan."

5. I know a man who makes deliveries for a foot doctor. He drives the toe truck.

6. Chubby husband: If I don't eat this food, it'll go to waste.
   Wife: And if you do eat it, it'll go to waist.

7. "What are the strongest days?"
   "Saturday and Sunday."
   "Why?"
   "Monday through Friday are weekdays."

8. What do they call the man who abandoned his strict diet?
   Desserter!

9. "Where did they fry the first French fries in history?"
   "In France?"
   "No, in grease."

10. What do grapes do when people step on them?
    They let out a little wine.

11. Lion: Never play cards with that spotted African wildcat.
Tiger: Why not?
Lion: He's a cheetah!

12. Delivery man: Should I deliver this coal to the cellar?
Boss: No, silly. To the buyer.

13. Doctor: What got you to my office so fast?
Patient: Flu.

14. Navy instructor: Your grades are all underwater.
Sailor: What do you mean?
Navy instructor: Below C-level.

15. Lady: How did you get that bump on your nose?
Neighbor: I tried to smell a brose in the garden.
Lady: You mean rose. There's no "b" in it.
Neighbor: There was in the one I was smelling!

16. Nurse: One of the doctors will see you now.
Patient: Which doctor?
Nurse: No, just a regular one.

17. Boy: What are those holes in the lumber?
Carpenter: Those are knotholes.
Boy: Well, they sure look like holes to me.

18. What did the Invisible Kid call his mom and dad?
Transparents.

19. "I help the carpenter. I pick up little nails."
"Oh, you're a tacks collector."

20. Teacher: How do you spell "This fish is blind"?
Student: T-H-S F-S-H S B-L-N-D.
Teacher: You left out four i's.
Student: If the fish had four eyes, it wouldn't be blind.

21. "Is that the Ambassador from Moscow dashing out the door?"
"Yes. He's always rushin'."

22. A man got a big increase in salary, so he sent his mother on a vacation. She spent two weeks on the beach enjoying the son's raise.

23. "Do your brothers have jobs?"
"Oh, yes. One smooths laundry. The other one robs."
"I see. They're in the iron and steel business."

24. Why did the nervous man sell his rabbit farm?
    He had too many hare-raising experiences.

25. Captain: Did you see that whale?
    Sailor 1: Aye, Captain!
    Captain: Who else saw it?
    Sailor 2: I, Captain!
    Captain: What about you?
    Sailor 3: I missed it.
    Captain: Why?
    Sailor 3: I have trouble with my eye, Captain.

Sound-Alike Words from Chapter 1

1. carrot (karat)
2. deer (dear)
3. Plains (planes)
4. maid (made)
5. toe (tow)
6. waist (waste)
7. week (weak)
8. desserter (deserter)
9. grease (Greece)
10. wine (whine)
11. cheetah (cheater)
12. cellar (seller)
13. flu (flew)
14. C (sea)
15. b (bee)
16. which (witch)
17. knot (not)
18. transparents (transparence)
19. tacks (tax)
20. i's (eyes)
21. rushin' (Russian)
22. son's (sun's); raise (rays)
23. steal (steel)
24. hare (hair)
25. aye, I, eye

Make Up Your Own

Now, try making up some homonym/homophone jokes and riddles of your own. Here are a dozen suggestions to get you started. Think of a setting in which you can substitute one sound-alike word for another to give your audience an unexpected chuckle. Ideas are suggested to help you put the words into settings. Now turn your imagination loose and see what jokes you can create.

Homonyms/Homophones	*The joke could be about*
hoarse (having a rough voice) horse (four-legged animal)	a horse shouting at a football game
whale (a huge sea mammal) wail (to cry and sob loudly)	a baby whale losing its favorite toy
flea (tiny insect) flee (to run away)	a flea escaping from the bug jail
hoes (garden tools) hose (stockings)	winter in the garden —the tools are cold
minor (underage person) miner (digs for coal)	a young coal digger
days (twenty-four-hour periods) daze (dizziness)	being dizzy for twenty-four-hour periods
heard (listened) herd (cattle)	what the cows listened to

Rome (capital of Italy)
roam (wander about)   wandering in Italy

knight (soldier in armor)
night (opposite of day)   fighting after dark

urn (vase)   getting a job
earn (getting a salary)   making vases

pain (physical suffering)
pane (window glass)   injured windows

knit (make sweaters)   an insect getting a
nit (tiny insect)   job in a sweater
                                       factory

°2°

Jokes with Almost-Sound-Alike Words

What do you call the dining car on a railroad?
The chew-chew train.

What do you call the train that delivers ballet skirts?
The tutu train.

Did you spot the play on homonym words in the jokes above? Of course: *choo-choo* and *chew-chew*. Did you also spot another play on words? Not homonyms, but almost-homonyms: *choo-choo* and *tutu*.

Sometimes what makes a joke funny is a word in it that *almost* sounds like another word—almost, but not quite. The words that almost sound alike must have different meanings.

As examples, here are two whale jokes.

What do you call a whale who can't stop talking?
A blubbermouth!

"I weigh whales."
"Where?"
"At a whale-weigh station."

Blubber almost sounds like *blabber*, and *whale-weigh* almost sounds like *railway*. And therein lie the laughs.

Here's how to make up jokes and riddles with words that almost sound like other words. First, think of a common word, any word, like *fur*. Next, think of words that almost sound like it, like *far* and *for*.

Now, let your imagination fly. Try to think of situations, settings, or contexts in which you could switch one almost-sound-alike word for another in a way that makes comical sense.

A comedian like you, after playing around with *fur*, *far*, and *for*, could come up with funny lines like these:

"How do you get fur from a tiger?"
"Run fast."

Customer: I'd like to buy a fur coat.
Salesperson: What fur?
Customer: Because it's cold outside!

Get the idea? Here's one last example just for practice. Think of a stork. Think of words that sound like *stork*—for instance, *stock* and *stalk* (note: the l is silent). Think of the comic possibilities of switching these words around. Storks bring babies. People invest in stocks and bonds. Plants grow on stalks. A little creative substituting might yield these jokes:

Baby Celery: Mama, where did I come from?
Mama Celery: The stalk brought you, dear.

A baby doctor makes his money on the stork market.

The rich celery farmer earned a fortune on the stalk market.

Your audience will laugh (or groan) when they hear those jokes and riddles and the ones that follow. Watch and listen for the words that almost sound like other words. They are revealed on page 31.

1. I hate reading poetry. It couldn't be verse.

2. What did the modest cow say when she won the "Most Milk" contest?
   "I owe it all to udders."

3. Teacher: What does your grandpa do for a living?
   Student: He don't do nothin'.
   Teacher: "Don't do nothin'"? What about your grammar?
   Student: She don't do nothin' neither.

4. It's raining cats and dogs outside. I almost stepped in a poodle!

5. What do you call spiders who just got married?
   Newlywebs.

6. "What should I use to polish a tuba?"
   "A tuba polish."

7. What do you get when you cross a rooster and a duck?
A bird that wakes you up at the quack of dawn.

8. Caller: I'd like to speak to the king of the jungle.
Zoo Operator: Sorry, sir. The lion is busy.

9. What do you get if you cross a cow and two ducks?
Milk and quackers.

10. What happened to the duck who flew upside down?
He quacked up!

11. Woodcutter: I need a new axe.
Wife: I'll put it on my chopping list.

12. Who fixes dolphin's piano?
    The piano tuna.

13. What did the slightly deaf fish wear in his ear?
    A herring aid.

14. School (of fish) teacher: Why did you bump into
    that dolphin?
    Fresh fish: I didn't do it on porpoise.

15. "What comes after 8-Q and 9-Q?"
    "10-Q."
    "You're welcome!"

16. Husband: Aghh! Aghh! I swallowed a chicken bone—sideways!!
    Wife: Are you choking?
    Husband: No. I'm serious!

17. Publisher: Why did you stop writing your long novel?
    Writer: My hand was hurting. I got authoritis.

18. "What do you call a pirate ship?"
    "A thug boat."

19. Friendly beaver to tree: It's been nice gnawing you.

20. Student: My mother is an Eskimo.
    Teacher: Where does she come from?
    Student: Alaska.
    Teacher: When she tells you, let me know.

21. Peter Pig: Boy, it's hot out. I never sausage heat.
    Patrick Pig: I know. I'm almost bacon!

22. A canary who was an opera singer had trouble with her voice. So she went to a throat doctor for special tweetment.

23. Why didn't the auto mechanic wash up before going to sleep?
    Because he wanted to get up oily in the morning.

24. Man 1: My new car broke down again.
    Man 2: They don't make cars like they auto.

25. "Can you telephone from a car?"
    "Sure! The phone has a dial. The car has wheels."

Almost-Sound-Alike Words
from Chapter 2

1.   *verse / worse*
2.   *udders / others*
3.   *grammar / grandma*
4.   *poodle / puddle*
5.   *webs / weds*
6.   *tuba / tube of*
7.   *quack / crack*
8.   *lion / line*
9.   *quackers / crackers*
10. *quacked / cracked*
11. *chopping / shopping*
12. *tuna / tuner*
13. *herring / hearing*
14. *porpoise / purpose*
15. *10-Q / thank you*
16. *choking / joking*
17. *authoritis / arthritis*
18. *thug / tug*
19. *gnawing / knowing*
20. *Alaska / I'll ask her*
21. *sausage / saw such; bacon / bakin'*
22. *tweetment / treatment*
23. *oily / early*
24. *auto / ought to*
25. *telephone / tell a phone*

Make Up Your Own

Now you might like to try making up jokes and riddles of your own using words that almost sound alike. Here are a dozen suggested punch lines. You make up the straight lines.

Almost-Sound-Alike Words	*The punch line could be*
muscle / missile	The spaceman was hit by a guided muscle.
fractions / actions	Fractions speak louder than words.
peas / peace	The fighting farmers held a peas conference.
boat / boot	A delivery ship for a shoe store.
crime / grime	They were arrested for the terrible grime.
rust / rest	Rust in peace!
haddock / headache	The fisherman had a splitting haddock.
banana / banner	The Star Spangled Banana!

clock / cluck

The cluck struck nine.

shoe / show

There's no business like shoe business.

aunt / ant

She's my ant!

lunch / lunge

The swordsmen went out for their lunge hour.

·3·

Jokes with Homographs

Headline: BAKERS ON STRIKE.
             THEY KNEAD MORE DOUGH.

Do you see the homonym in the punch line of the joke above? Right—*knead/need.* But there's another play on words in that joke. *Dough* is a word with two different meanings. It can mean the flour mixture bread is made from. It is also a slang word for money.

Dough and *dough* are homographs. Homographs are words that are spelled alike, and sound alike, but mean different things.

Homographs can confuse you, because if you don't hear or see the word in a sentence, you don't know what its specific meaning is.

For instance, what do you think of when you read or hear the word *conductor*? Here's a sentence with three "conductors" in it: The orchestra conductor told the train conductor that copper is a good conductor of electricity. All those "conductors" are homographs: words that have the same spelling and pronunciation but different meanings.

To make up jokes and riddles with homographs, you substitute one meaning of a homograph for another meaning in a way that's unexpected but actually makes a funny kind of sense.

For example, consider three different definitions of *racket*: a loud, unpleasant noise; a hand-held device used to hit a ball in a sport like tennis; a slang word for a business, job, or profession.

Now, by switching meanings for *racket* you can create jokes like these:

"What do you do for a living?"
"I play professional tennis."
"Oh, I see. You're in the tennis racket."

Tennis is a very noisy game. The players are always raising a racket.

There are lots of additional possibilities for joke-making with *racket*. Tennis players put cotton in their ears because they can't stand the racket. A manufacturer of expensive tennis equipment has quite a racket going for him. Gangsters who play tennis could be called racketeers. Get the idea?

Here's another exercise in making jokes with homographs. *Sentence* has two common meanings: a group of words and a punishment for a crime. Try playing around with those meanings and you might come up with homograph jokes like these:

My English teacher is like a judge. She's always handing out sentences.

What's the longest sentence in the world?
Life imprisonment!

Lawyer: Your honor, please give my client a short
sentence.
Judge: He gets ten years in jail.
Lawyer: That's not a short sentence.
Judge: Yes it is. It has only six words!

Speaking of judges, what's your verdict on this joke?

Judge: I sentence you to spend one night in jail.
Crook: What's the charge?
Judge: No charge. The cell is free.

That joke works because *charge* means both the accusation of a crime ("What's the charge, officer?") and the cost of something ("No charge").

Charge can also mean: to put off paying for something until a later time ("I'll charge that"), to rush ahead violently ("The general shouted, 'Charge!' "), and to supply with electrical energy ("The car battery needs to be charged").

All of that leads us to these two charged-up jokes:

How do you charge a battery?
With your credit card.

What did the elephant with no money do at the shopping mall?
Charge!

Now let's charge ahead to more examples of homograph jokes. This time we'll use three different meanings of *spring*: a little river, a season of the year, and a coiled metal device that returns to its original shape after being pushed down.

"I sleep in my bed only in the summer, fall, and winter."
"Why?"
"It has no spring."

"Those two bedbugs are really in love."
"Yes. They're getting married in the spring."

Did you hear about the man who almost drowned in his bed?
His mattress was ripped, and he fell into the spring.

Country boy: I take baths in the spring.
City boy: What do you do in the other seasons, take showers?

Diner: Waiter, this lamb is very tough to chew.
Waiter: Sir, that's a spring lamb.
Diner: Well, I think I'm chewing on the spring.

Which "spring" joke is the funniest? You be the judge.

Now we'll spring to one last example of joke-making with homographs. *Nut* can mean a seed with a hard shell, a crazy person, and a small block of metal with a threaded hole.

Here are three nutty jokes:

In my school cafeteria, they serve soup to nuts.

It's not a loose bolt that makes a car unsafe, it's the nut behind the wheel.

Principal (at lunch): Will you pass the nuts?
Angry Teacher: No. I'm going to fail them all.

In the last joke, did you notice *two* pairs of homographs: *pass* (opposite of fail / to hand over) and *nuts* (weird people / fruits with hard shells)?

Here's another joke with two homograph switches in it. Can you spot both of them?

Salesperson: Here's a nice jacket for you.
Customer: Don't you think it's kind of loud?
Salesperson: Not if you wear it with a muffler.

Since there are thousands of homographs in English, there are thousands of opportunities to create jokes and riddles with them. Here's a sampling.

1. "Do you want to see the new show at the planetarium?"
   "I like only shows with celebrities in them."
   "Well, this is an all-star show."

2. Headline: MAN FALLS
   INTO EYEGLASS MACHINE
   MAKES SPECTACLE OF HIMSELF!

3. The leopard tried to escape from his cage, but he was spotted.

4. Father: Money doesn't grow on trees, you know!
   Son: Then why does the bank have so many branches?

5. Grandma (in restaurant): I feel like a bowl of spaghetti.
   Waiter: Funny, you look like a little old lady.

6. "Why did you name your dog Tick-Tock?"
   "He's a watchdog."

7. Sports headline:
   KITTEN WINS MILK-DRINKING CONTEST
   BY THREE LAPS!

8. Daughter: Mommy, there's a strange-looking man at the door.
   Mother: Does he have a bill?
   Daughter: No, just a regular nose.

9. Art Teacher: Class, draw a horse and cart.
   Lazy Student: I'll draw the horse. The horse can draw the cart.

10. Boy: Do you notice any change in me?
    Doctor (looking at X-ray): No.
    Boy: You should. I swallowed two dimes and a nickel.

11. Forest Ranger: Class, what is the outside of a tree
    called?
    Boy: The trunk?
    Ranger: No.
    Girl: The limbs?
    Ranger: No.
    Class: We give up.
    Ranger: Bark, class, bark.
    Class: Bow wow! Woof woof!

12. Customer: Waitress, this coffee tastes just like dirt!
    Waitress: It should. It was ground a few minutes ago.

13. Boy: What do you make shoes with?
    Shoemaker: Hide.
    Boy: What for? Nobody's chasing me.
    Shoemaker: No. Hide. The cow's outside.
    Boy: Tell her to come in. I'm not afraid of her.

14. "Mom, why does the tooth fairy give me only a quarter when Sally gets a dollar?"
    "Because Sally has buck teeth."

15. Brother: These drops make my eyes smart.
    Sister: Quick, rub some on your head!

16. Auto mechanic: How did you get this flat tire?
    Driver: There was a fork in the road.

17. Bill said, "Look at that duck."
    Phil said, "That's a swan, not a duck."
    "Duck," insisted Bill.
    "Swan," insisted Phil.
    All of a sudden, a low-flying goose was heading straight for Phil.
    "Duck!" shouted Bill.
    "Swan!" shouted Phil and got conked in the head by the goose.

18. Why does it take a baseball player so long to run from second base to third?
Because there's a short stop in between.

19. "Is business picking up on your duck feather farm?"
"No, it's picking down."

20. Judge: You must pay fifty dollars for parking in the wrong place.
Driver: But the sign said it was OK to park there.
Judge: It did?
Driver: Sure. It said "Fine for Parking."

21. My uncle tells people he's a diamond cutter. He mows the grass at the baseball stadium.

22. Track Coach 1: How do you make a slow runner fast?
    Track Coach 2: Stop feeding him.

23. A long-distance runner broke his leg. His doctor told him that the leg would never be right. "Why not?" asked the runner.
    "Because it's your left leg!" said the doctor.

24. Teacher: Why can a person's hand never be longer than eleven inches?
    Student: Because if it were twelve inches, it would be a foot!

25. Did you hear about the man who went bear hunting? Driving in the woods, he saw a sign that said "Bear Left," so he went home.

Homographs from Chapter 3

1. star: bright light in the sky / famous performer
2. spectacle: eyeglasses / weird behavior in public
3. spotted: marked by spots / seen
4. branches: what grow out of trees / offices away from main building
5. feel: to be in the mood for / to have a particular texture and form
6. watch: to keep guard over / a time-telling device
7. laps: lengths of a pool / quick sips with the tongue
8. bill: paper stating what you owe / duck's beak
9. draw: to create a picture / to pull or drag
10. change: something different / coins
11. bark: outer covering of a tree / sound a dog makes
12. ground: soil, dirt / crushed into small pieces
13. hide: skin of an animal / to conceal
14. buck: dollar (slang) / sticking out (said of teeth)
15. smart: to sting / intelligent
16. fork: eating utensil / place where a road divides
17. duck: a web-footed waterfowl / to lower the head
18. short stop: brief pause / player between second and third base
19. down: opposite of up / soft duck feathers
20. fine: money paid as punishment / very good
21. diamond: precious stone / baseball infield
22. fast: moving quickly / to not eat
23. right: healthy or normal / opposite of left
24. foot: the bottom of your leg / twelve inches
25. bear: large animal / turn in the direction of
26. left: departed / opposite of right

Make Up Your Own

Now try making up homograph jokes of your own. You can find homographs everywhere—in dictionaries, newspapers, magazines, books. It might be a good idea to keep your own list of homographs so you'll be ready when the joke-making spirit strikes you. Here are a dozen words with multiple meanings that you can use:

Homographs	*The punch line could be*
point (sharp end / meaning)	It doesn't have a point.
stumps (bottoms of trees / puzzles)	Stumps me!
bright (giving off light / smart)	Her students were so bright.
jerk (sharp pull / foolish person)	Any little jerk can do it.

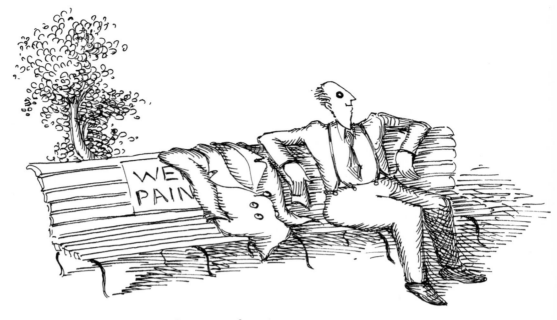

coat (clothing / layer of paint)

I gave it two coats.

cast (actors / covering for broken limb)

He was in the cast.

vessel (part of circulatory system / ship)

It's a vampire's boat!

relish (pickles / delight)

He ate it with relish.

trunk (elephant's nose / big suitcase)

In its trunk.

scales (covering of fish skin / musical notes)

It had to learn its scales.

batter (baseball player / cake dough)

Batter up!

fan (breeze maker / enthusiastic admirer)

That's my biggest fan.

∘4∘

Jokes with Idioms

There are thousands of expressions in English that have unexpected meanings. The meaning of the saying as a whole might not have anything to do with the meaning of each of the words in the saying.

For example, people sometimes say, "Don't let the cat out of the bag." The meaning of the expression ("Don't reveal the secret") actually has nothing to do with a cat or a bag.

Here's another example. A person in the mood to go out and have a good time might say, "I'm going to paint the town red." He really doesn't mean, of course, that he's going to get a paintbrush and a bucket of red paint and start changing the color of the buildings.

These tricky expressions are called idioms. You hear, read, and use idioms every day. Here are some more common ones:

He put his foot in his mouth. (He said something he shouldn't have.)

That's a feather in your cap. (That's a great accomplishment.)

Hold your horses! (Slow down. Don't rush ahead.)
Are you pulling my leg? (Are you trying to fool me?)

You can use idioms to make up jokes and riddles just as you can use homonyms, almost-homonyms, and homographs. For instance, "having cold feet" means being afraid to do something. It has nothing to do with the temperature of your feet. To turn this idiom into a joke, try to think of someone who really might have cold feet. What about a snowman or a barefoot skier? What would he be afraid of doing? The punch line is going to be about cold feet. Here's the outline of the joke:

Straight line:
Why didn't _____ _____?
                (the cold person) (do something)

Punch line: _____ cold feet!

Fill in the blanks and it might come out like this:

Why didn't the abominable snowman ask the girl for a date?
He got cold feet!

52

Speaking of feet (if the joke above leaves you cold), do you know what "sweeping someone off his feet" means? It isn't something you do with a broom. It means wowing someone, making him or her fall in love with you. In order to make up a joke with this idiom, you have to think of someone who really does sweep. Then think up a situation in which that person makes someone fall in love with her or him. Here's one example:

"Why did the millionaire marry the cleaning lady?"
"She swept him off his feet."

While we're on the subject of love, when people are "head over heels in love" it just means they're very, very much in love. They won't be doing flips; their feet will still be firmly planted on the ground. But what kind of people really do flip over? Acrobats, of course. Think of acrobats in love and you might come up with jokes like these:

Did you hear about the romantic acrobats who were head over heels in love with each other?

or

Did you hear about the trapeze artist who fell head over heels in love with the acrobat?

Here are more jokes that use common idioms in un-expected and funny ways.

1. "I've changed my mind."
   "Good, I hope your new one works better than your old one."

2. Student: How did I do on my report card?
   Teacher: The same as Abraham Lincoln.
   Student: Huh?
   Teacher: You went down in history.

3. "My older brother beats me up every morning."
   "That's awful."
   "Not really. He gets up at seven thirty. I get up at eight."

4. "Why do you wear two pair of pants to the golf course?"
   "In case I get a hole in one!"

5. Nurse: I'm going to take your pulse.
   Patient: Please don't keep it long. I need it myself.

6. Stranger: Do the trains in this town run on time?
   Old-timer: Nope. They run on tracks.

7. Elevator operator: Tenth floor. All out, my children.
   Passengers: Why do you call us your children?
   Elevator operator: I brought you all up, didn't I?

8. Teacher: Why are you so sleepy in class today?
   Boy: I was awakened early this morning by a loud noise.
   Teacher: What was it?
   Boy: The crack of dawn.
   Teacher: Is that why your brother is so sleepy too?
   Boy: No, he heard the break of day.

9. "Why is the calendar crying?"
   "Its days are numbered."

10. Man: Will you marry me?
    Woman: Sure, if you give me a ring.
    Man: OK. What's your phone number?

11. Lady 1: Whenever I'm down in the dumps, I buy myself a new dress.
    Lady 2: So that's where you get them.

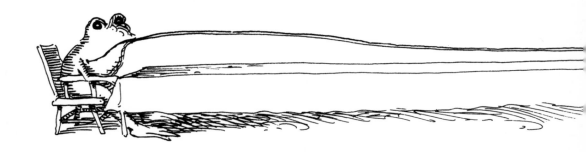

12. Aunt: Stop reaching for food across the table.
Haven't you got a tongue?
Nephew: Sure. But my arm's longer.

13. Census Taker: How old are you?
Miss Jones: I'm not telling.
Census Taker: Everyone has to tell.
Miss Jones: Did the Hill twins next door tell?
Census Taker: They certainly did.
Miss Jones: Well, I was born the same year as
they were.
Census Taker: I see. You're as old as the Hills.

14. Why is the deep-sea diver always so sad?
Because every day his friends let him down.

15. An ancient astronomer once stayed up all night
trying to figure out where the sun had gone.
In the morning it dawned on him.

16. Why did the man in the expensive clothes get hired?
    He was well suited for the job.

17. Bill: (crying) I just got fired. My career lies in ruins.
    Phil: (laughing) Mine too.
    Bill: Then why are you so happy?
    Phil: I'm an archaeologist!

18. Athletic coach: What sports do you like?
    Student: Well, I get a kick out of soccer, and bowling is right up my alley.

19. Did you hear about the bad boy who brought his toy truck to school so he could drive his teacher up the wall?

20. Who never cries over spilled milk?
    A cat.

21. Girl: This is a picture of my grandmother.
    Teacher: Is she on your mother's side or your father's side?
    Girl: Neither. She always sticks up for me.

22. Why did the skeleton quit his job?
    Because his heart wasn't in it.

23. Policeman 1: Who was the biggest crook in history?
    Policeman 2: Atlas. He held up the whole world.

24. "Ma, may I have a dollar for being good?"
    "Certainly not. You should be good for nothing!"

25. Customer: Can you please help me out?
    Salesperson: Certainly. Which way did you come in?

Idioms from Chapter 4

1. changed my mind: arrived at a different opinion
2. went down in history: became famous
3. beats me up: awakens before I do
4. hole in one: get the golf ball into the hole with only one shot
5. take your pulse: find out how fast your heart is beating
6. run on time: arrive and depart on schedule
7. brought you up: raised you from childhood
8. crack of dawn, break of day: the moment when the sun rises
9. days are numbered: doesn't have long to live
10. give me a ring: call me up on the phone
11. down in the dumps: feeling very depressed
12. got a tongue: are able to speak
13. old as the hills: ancient
14. let him down: disappoint him
15. dawned on him: occurred to him
16. well suited: perfectly qualified
17. in ruins: completely destroyed
18. get a kick out of: enjoy something a lot
    right up my alley: just perfect for me
19. drive up the wall: annoy and irritate greatly
20. cries over spilled milk: complains about something that can't be fixed
21. on your side: supports you
22. heart wasn't in it: didn't really care about it
23. held up: robbed, usually at gunpoint
24. good for nothing: totally worthless
25. help me out: assist me

Make Up Your Own

Now it's your turn to make up your own jokes and riddles, this time using idioms. Below you will find a bunch of common sayings and some suggestions for how they could be used in jokes.

Idioms	*The joke/riddle could be about*
catching forty winks	a sleepy baseball player
raising the roof	an angry demolition worker
giving someone the cold shoulder	an unfriendly snowman
hitting the hay	a tired farmhand or cow

kicking the bucket	a clumsy milkmaid or cow
getting into someone's hair	a clumsy barber
walking on air (or clouds)	a skydiver or balloonist in love
shooting the breeze	a bow and arrow contest
by the skin of one's teeth	a dentist's narrow escape
straight from the horse's mouth	a veterinarian gets a tip
being a stuffed shirt	a important chubby man
burying your head in the sand	kids hiding from bully at beach
getting up on the wrong side of the bed	dangerous sleepwalking
giving someone a piece of your mind	an angry robot
monkeying around with something	a curious monkey on the loose
throwing one's weight around	an important elephant or hippo

○5○

Where Did All These Jokes Come From?

You may be wondering where all the jokes in this book came from. Funny you should ask.

I made a lot of them up myself. My two children, David and Jennifer, and my wife, Karen, told me many of them. So did the students in my English classes. My uncle is a professional comedian and he always tries new jokes out on me. I remembered some jokes from my own childhood, and I've always enjoyed reading joke books.

Everyone enjoys a good joke. Tell a good joke and people will say, "Thanks very much."

Or as the army general would say, "Tanks very much."

Or as the trickster would say, "Pranks very much."

Or as the hot-dog seller would say, "Franks very much."

Or as the carpenter would say, "Planks very much."

Or as the millionaire would say, "Banks very much."

Or as the naughty child would say, "Spanks very much."

Or as the skunk would say, "Stanks very much."

More Joke and Riddle Books

If you haven't read enough jokes yet, you could go to your school or public library or your local bookstore and get some more. Here are some books that the author read while writing this book.

Kilgariff, Michael. *1,000 Jokes for Kids of All Ages.* New York: Ballantine Books, 1974.

———. *1,000 More Jokes for Kids.* New York: Ballantine Books, 1982.

Maestro, Giulio. *What's a Frank Frank? Tasty Homograph Riddles.* New York: Clarion Books, 1984.

Rosenbloom, Joseph. *The Gigantic Joke Book.* New York: Sterling Publishing Co., Inc., 1978.

———. *696 Silly School Jokes & Riddles.* New York: Sterling Publishing Co., Inc., 1986.

Terban, Marvin. *Eight Ate: A Feast of Homonym Riddles.* New York: Clarion Books, 1982.

———. *Hey, Hay! A Wagonful of Funny Homonym Riddles.* New York: Clarion Books, 1990.

———. *In a Pickle: And Other Funny Idioms.* New York: Clarion Books, 1983.

———. *Mad as a Wet Hen! And Other Funny Idioms.* New York: Clarion Books, 1987.

———. *Punching the Clock: Funny Action Idioms.* New York: Clarion Books, 1989.